The Heinemann Illustrated Encyclopedia

Index

First published in Great Britain by Heinemann Library
Halley Court, Jordan Hill, Oxford OX2 8EJ
a division of Reed Educational and Professional Publishing Ltd.

OXFORD MELBOURNE AUCKLAND
JOHANNESBURG BLANTYRE GABORONE
IBADAN PORTSMOUTH NH (USA) CHICAGO

Series Editors: Rebecca and Stephen Vickers
Author Team: Rob Alcraft, Catherine Chambers, Jim Drake,
Fred Martin, Angela Royston, Jane Shuter, Roger Thomas,
Rebecca Vickers, Stephen Vickers
Reading Consultant: Betty Root

Photo research by Katharine Smith
Designed and Typeset by Gecko Ltd
Illustrations by Joanne Cowne and David Mostyn. Maps by Oxford Illustrators.
Printed in Hong Kong by Wing King Tong

02 01 00 99 98
10 9 8 7 6 5 4 3 2 1

ISBN 0 431 09063 7

British Library Cataloguing in Publication Data.

The Heinemann illustrated encyclopedia
1. Children's encyclopedias and dictionaries
I. Vickers, Rebecca II. Vickers, Stephen, 1951–
032

ISBN 0431090629

Contents

A world of countries

This is a map of all the countries in the world. It shows the lines where one country finishes, and the next begins. These lines are called borders.

Some borders between countries follow rivers or mountains. Other borders are straight lines. They can divide people who speak the same language, or live in the same way.

As you look at it remember that the world is really round like an orange. This map is like the Earth's skin flattened out. It makes it easier to look at on a page, but does make some countries look bigger than they really are. For instance Greenland is not really as big as it looks. South America should look a little bigger.

THE TEN BIGGEST COUNTRIES

RUSSIA	17,075,000
CANADA	9,976,140
CHINA	9,596,960
USA	9,372,610
BRAZIL	8,511,970
AUSTRALIA	7,686,850
INDIA	3,287,590
ARGENTINA	2,776,890
KAZAKSTAN	2,717,300
SUDAN	2,505,810

Numbers are in square kms.

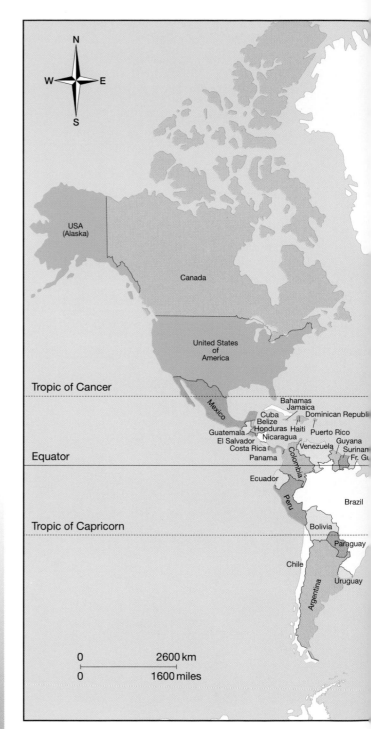

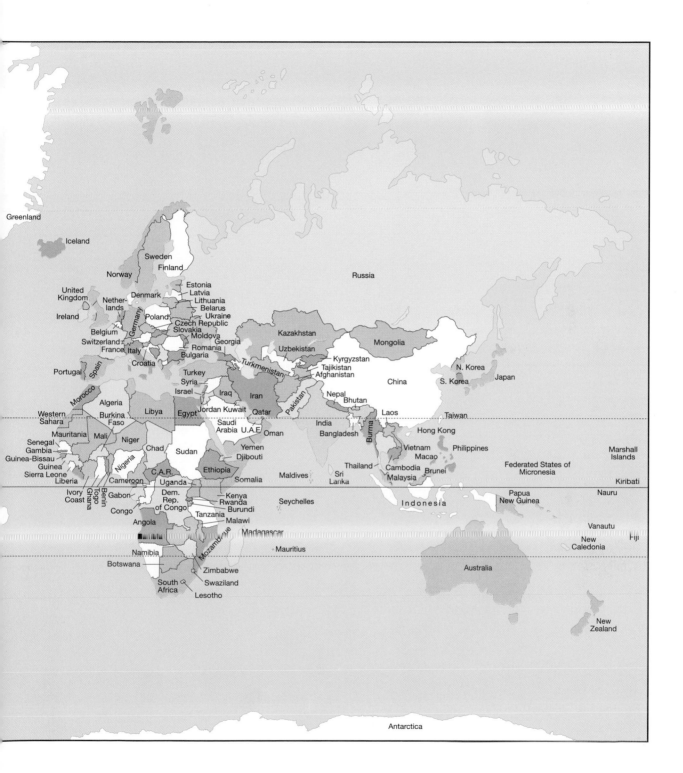

Land and sea

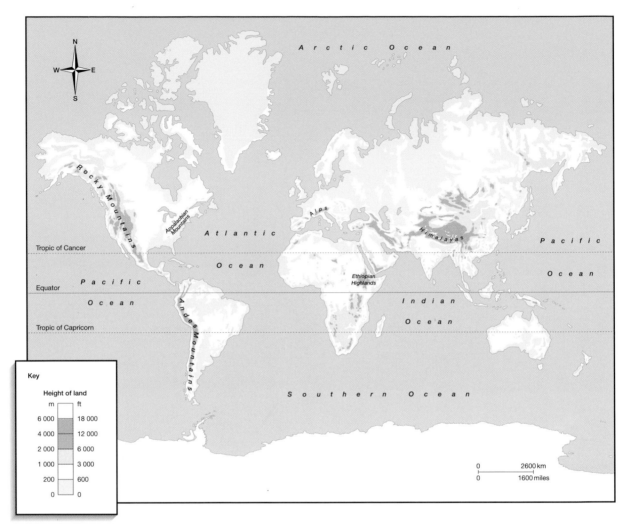

This is a map of the world which shows water and the height of the land. You can see that most of the world's surface is ocean and sea.

Only a quarter of the world is land. There are mountains, which on this map are shown as shadowed areas. Mountains are made where the land has become crumpled, just like a giant paper bag being screwed up. The highest mountains are in the Himalayas, in Asia.

The world's deserts, where it is hot and dry, are usually in low areas.

Much of Australia is desert. Africa has the world's largest desert, called the Sahara.

LAND AND SEA FACTS

HIGHEST MOUNTAIN... Mount Everest, 8848m, Himalayas

DEEPEST PLACE IN THE OCEAN .... Mariana Trench in the Pacific Ocean, 11,022m

LONGEST RIVER .... Nile, Africa

BIGGEST DESERT .... Sahara, Africa

Where people live

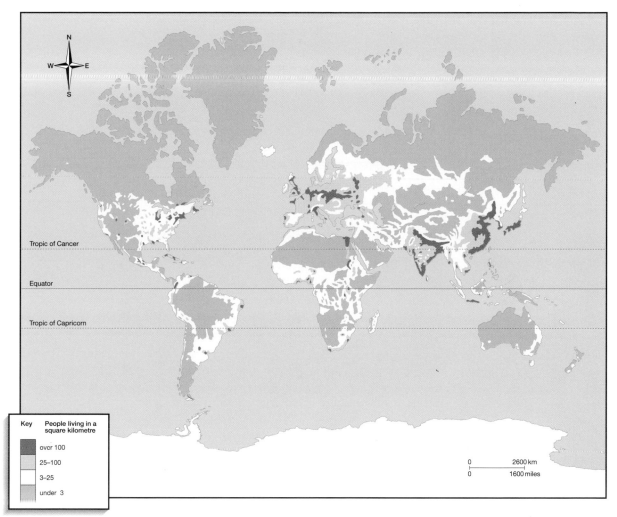

Key — People living in a square kilometre

- over 100
- 25–100
- 3–25
- under 3

Tropic of Cancer

Equator

Tropic of Capricorn

| 0 | 2600 km |
| 0 | 1600 miles |

This is a map of the world which shows where people live.

Most of the world has few people. These areas are coloured pale blue. In some of these places it is too cold to live easily. Some of it is desert, and too hot and dry to grow food. Very few people live in the world's high mountains.

The brown colours show where the greatest number of people live. They live in the low land areas of the world. Here there is rain, and good land to grow food.

Over half the world's people live in the low lands of India and East Asia. Europe also has many people. The most crowded places are the big cities.

POPULATION FACTS

LARGEST CITY....... Tokyo in Japan, with 25 million people

COUNTRY WITH
MOST PEOPLE......... China has 1179 million people

Hot and cold: January

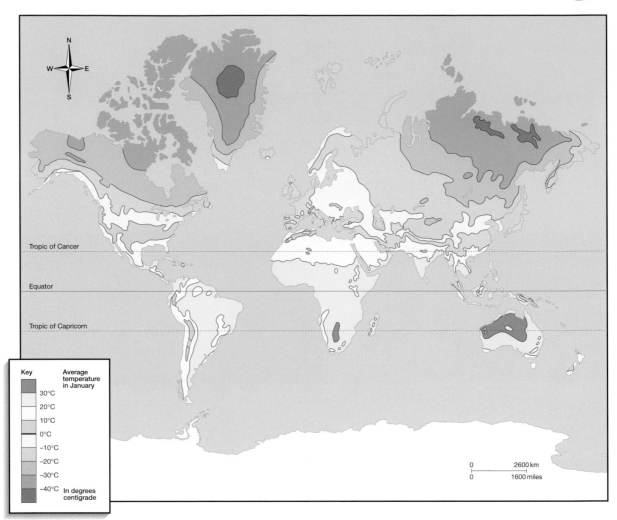

Key — Average temperature in January

- 30°C
- 20°C
- 10°C
- 0°C
- −10°C
- −20°C
- −30°C
- −40°C — In degrees centigrade

Tropic of Cancer

Equator

Tropic of Capricorn

0 — 2600 km
0 — 1600 miles

This is a map of the world in January. This is the time of year when the northern half of the world is furthest away from the Sun. This means that for these countries the days are short, and it is cold.

In the far north, the sun does not shine at all. It is dark all day, and very, very cold. For northern countries such as Sweden and Canada, it is cold and wintery. These places are very cold. On the map they are coloured in pale grey.

Most of the warm places in this January map are in the south. In places like Australia and South Africa, it is summer. The weather is hot, and the days are long.

WET AND DRY

WETTEST
PLACE......... Tutunendo in Colombia is the wettest. It has 11m of rain a year.

DRIEST
PLACE......... Atacama Desert in Chile. It hasn't rained there for 400 years.

Hot and cold: July

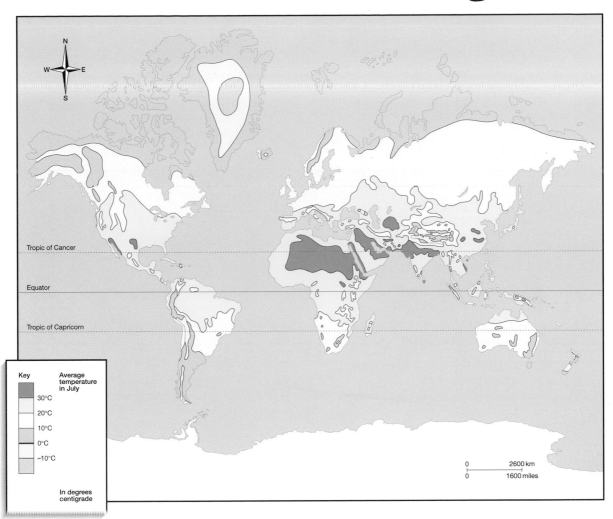

Key — Average temperature in July
- 30°C
- 20°C
- 10°C
- 0°C
- −10°C

In degrees centigrade

Tropic of Cancer

Equator

Tropic of Capricorn

0 — 2600 km
0 — 1600 miles

This is a map of the world in July. This is when northern countries are closest to the sun. In Britain and Canada it is summer. The days become longer, and the weather is warm.

In the far north, the Sun never goes down. There is day light all the time, although there is still snow and ice.

Compare this map to the one on the opposite page. Can you see that there are very few cold places in July?

In July the only really cold places are in the far north, and far south. In the very high mountains it is always cold, too.

HOT AND COLD

HOTTEST PLACE .... The hottest temperature that anyone has recorded is 58°C, in Al Azizyah in Libya.

COLDEST PLACE .... The coldest temperature anyone has recorded is −89°C at Vostok in Antarctica.

A world of plants

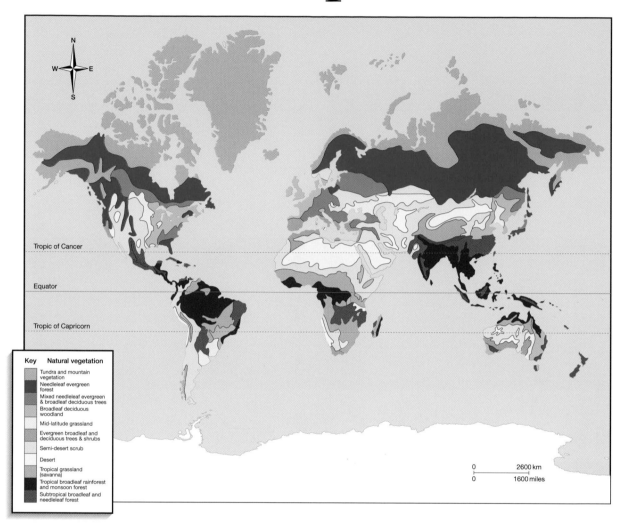

Key Natural vegetation

Tundra and mountain vegetation
Needleleaf evergreen forest
Mixed needleleaf evergreen & broadleaf deciduous trees
Broadleaf deciduous woodland
Mid-latitude grassland
Evergreen broadleaf and deciduous trees & shrubs
Semi-desert scrub
Desert
Tropical grassland (savanna)
Tropical broadleaf rainforest and monsoon forest
Subtropical broadleaf and needleleaf forest

Tropic of Cancer

Equator

Tropic of Capricorn

0   2600 km
0   1600 miles

This map shows the kinds of plants that grow around the world. Different plants grow depending on how cold or hot it is, or how wet or dry.

Plants grow best where the weather is always hot and wet. We call these places tropical. On the map they are dark green. The plants can grow all year. There is hot sun, and lots of rain.

In North America and Europe there is plenty of rain for plants, but it is much cooler. There are seasons. Many plants grow only in summer. In winter they drop their leaves.

In places where it is very dry, or very cold, few plants can grow. These are places like deserts, which are coloured yellow on the map.

Plant classification

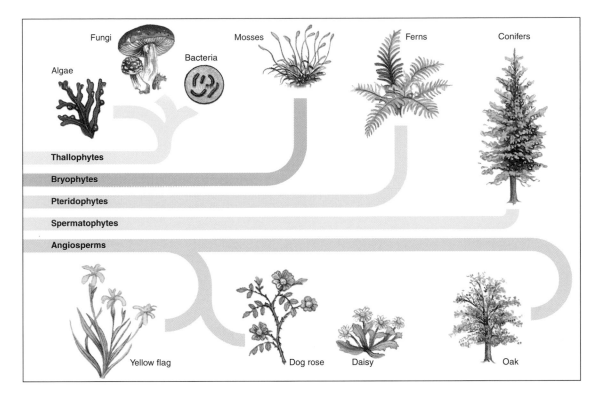

Fungi

Bacteria

Algae

Mosses

Ferns

Conifers

Thallophytes

Bryophytes

Pteridophytes

Spermatophytes

Angiosperms

Yellow flag

Dog rose

Daisy

Oak

Animal classification

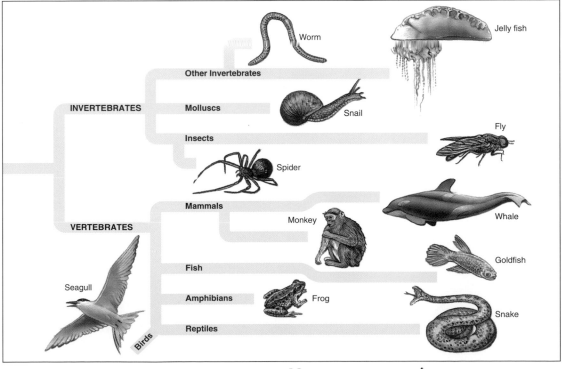

Worm

Jelly fish

Other Invertebrates

INVERTEBRATES

Molluscs

Snail

Insects

Fly

Spider

Mammals

Monkey

Whale

VERTEBRATES

Fish

Goldfish

Seagull

Amphibians

Frog

Snake

Birds

Reptiles

World history up to 1900

These pages shows some of the events during 5000 years of the world's history. Your great-great-grandparents were born in the years on the far right of these pages. On the far left page, no one can be completely sure what happened.

DINOSAURS 150,000,000 YEARS

TO THE MODERN WORLD

3000 BC
World population is about 80 million.

563 BC
The Buddha is born in India.

2800 BC
Stonehenge is built.

725 BC
First clock invented in China.

2575 BC
Great Pyramids begun in Egypt.

753 BC
The city of Rome is founded.

2500 BC
Aborigines living in Australia.

776 BC
First Olympic Games held in Greece.

2500 BC
China using bronze tools.

2250 BC
First map is made in Sumeria (now Iraq).

1300 BC
Olmec people build pyramids in Mexico.

2000 BC
Minoan civilization in Crete at its peak.

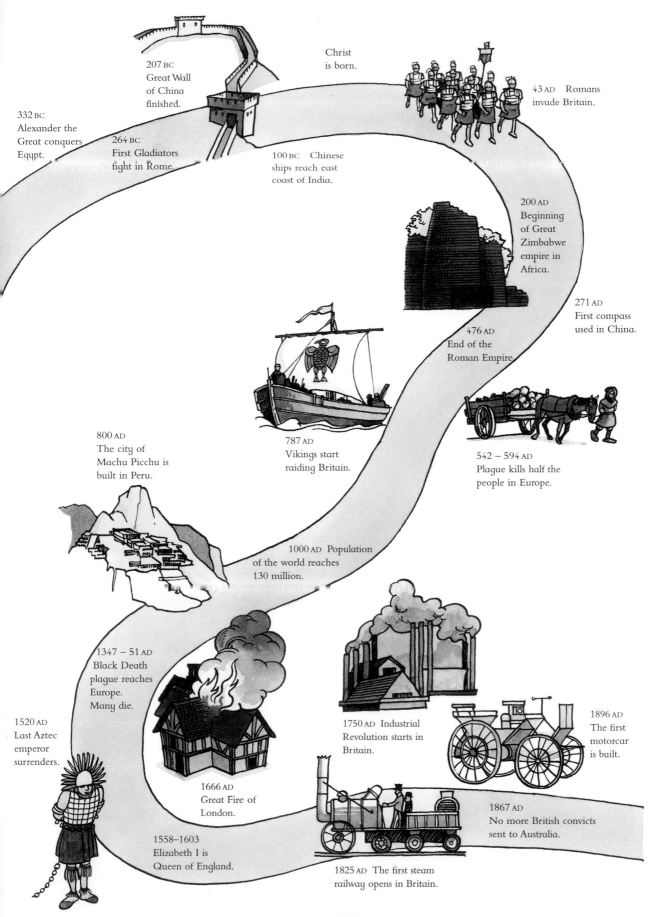

332 BC Alexander the Great conquers Egypt.

207 BC Great Wall of China finished.

264 BC First Gladiators fight in Rome.

100 BC Chinese ships reach east coast of India.

Christ is born.

43 AD Romans invade Britain.

200 AD Beginning of Great Zimbabwe empire in Africa.

271 AD First compass used in China.

476 AD End of the Roman Empire.

542 – 594 AD Plague kills half the people in Europe.

787 AD Vikings start raiding Britain.

800 AD The city of Machu Picchu is built in Peru.

1000 AD Population of the world reaches 130 million.

1347 – 51 AD Black Death plague reaches Europe. Many die.

1520 AD Last Aztec emperor surrenders.

1666 AD Great Fire of London.

1558–1603 Elizabeth I is Queen of England.

1750 AD Industrial Revolution starts in Britain.

1896 AD The first motorcar is built.

1867 AD No more British convicts sent to Australia.

1825 AD The first steam railway opens in Britain.

20th century world history

On these pages are some of the things that have happened in the 20th century. The year in which you were born is to the far right of the page. The furthest to the right is where we are now. Do you recognize any of the things that have happened in history?

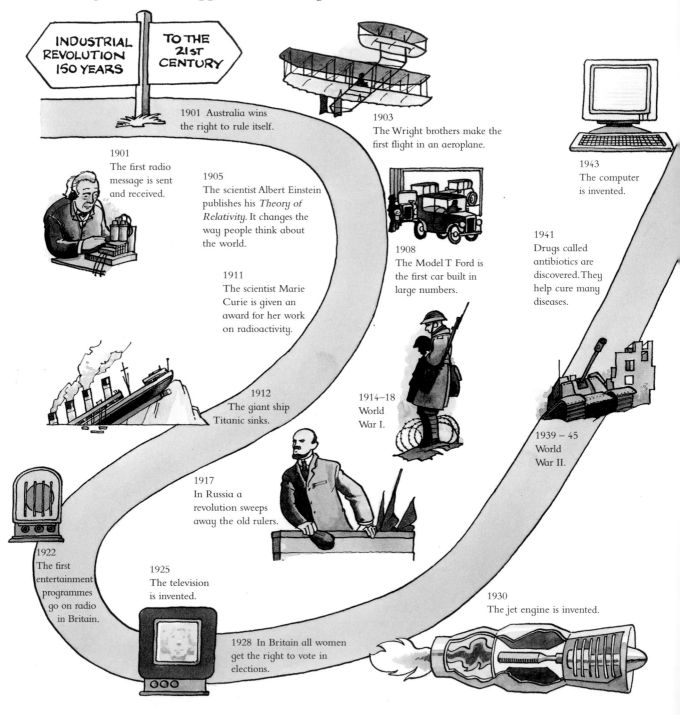

INDUSTRIAL REVOLUTION 150 YEARS

TO THE 21ST CENTURY

1901 Australia wins the right to rule itself.

1901 The first radio message is sent and received.

1903 The Wright brothers make the first flight in an aeroplane.

1943 The computer is invented.

1905 The scientist Albert Einstein publishes his *Theory of Relativity*. It changes the way people think about the world.

1908 The Model T Ford is the first car built in large numbers.

1941 Drugs called antibiotics are discovered. They help cure many diseases.

1911 The scientist Marie Curie is given an award for her work on radioactivity.

1912 The giant ship Titanic sinks.

1914–18 World War I.

1939 – 45 World War II.

1917 In Russia a revolution sweeps away the old rulers.

1922 The first entertainment programmes go on radio in Britain.

1925 The television is invented.

1930 The jet engine is invented.

1928 In Britain all women get the right to vote in elections.

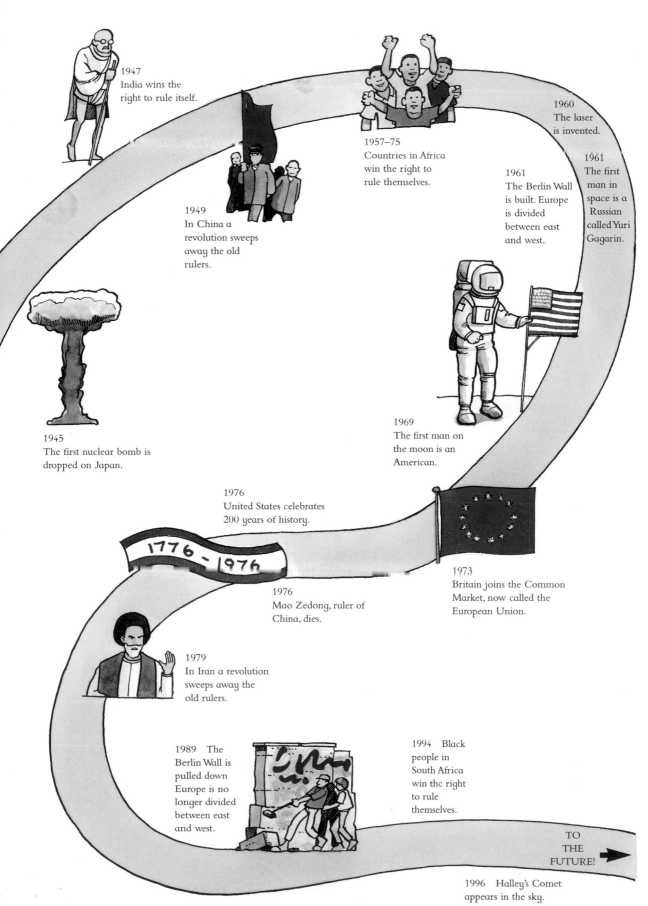

1947
India wins the right to rule itself.

1957–75
Countries in Africa win the right to rule themselves.

1960
The laser is invented.

1961
The Berlin Wall is built. Europe is divided between east and west.

1961
The first man in space is a Russian called Yuri Gagarin.

1949
In China a revolution sweeps away the old rulers.

1945
The first nuclear bomb is dropped on Japan.

1969
The first man on the moon is an American.

1976
United States celebrates 200 years of history.

1776 - 1976

1976
Mao Zedong, ruler of China, dies.

1973
Britain joins the Common Market, now called the European Union.

1979
In Iran a revolution sweeps away the old rulers.

1989   The Berlin Wall is pulled down. Europe is no longer divided between east and west.

1994   Black people in South Africa win the right to rule themselves.

TO THE FUTURE!

1996   Halley's Comet appears in the sky.

A world of stars

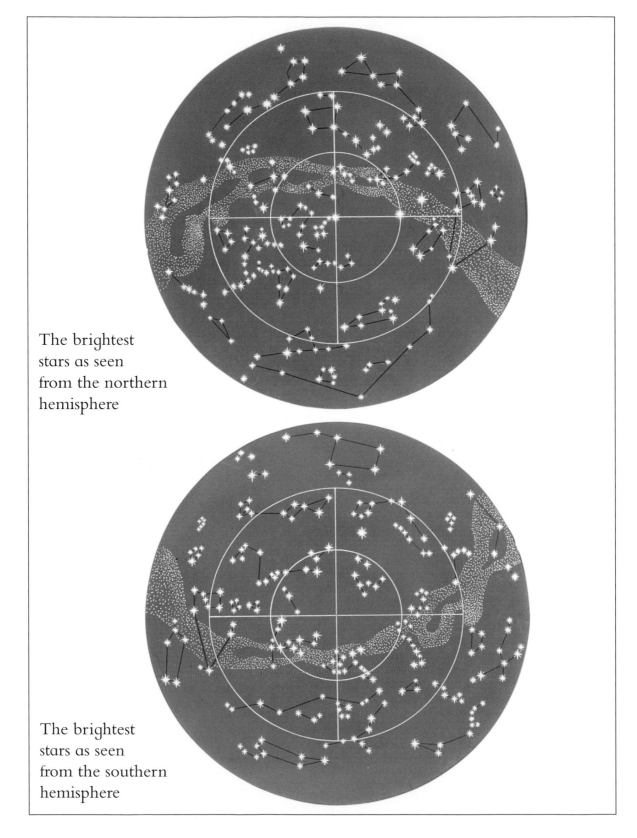

The brightest
stars as seen
from the northern
hemisphere

The brightest
stars as seen
from the southern
hemisphere

How to use this index

The index of the *Heinemann Illustrated Encyclopedia* is divided into two parts.

The Subject Index (pages 18–22)

The Subject Index lists all entry words in the encyclopedia grouped together in alphabetical (A–Z) order under a subject heading. For example, under the subject heading DINOSAURS you will find a list of all of the different dinosaur entries in the whole encyclopedia. The ANIMALS subject list is also divided into types of animals, such as mammals, birds and fish. The COUNTRIES entries are listed under the continent each country is found in. The main subject headings are in Dewey Decimal order, the order that books are arranged in most libraries.

The Alphabetic Index (pages 23–32)

The Alphabetic Index lists all the entry words in the encyclopedia and also some other important words. It tells you the page and volume number of the encyclopedia where information can be found. Some of the indexed words have *see also* references. These tell you other words to look under in the index to find more information. If the word you look under does not have page and volume information, there will be a *see* reference to tell you where to look.

Find the initial letter of the word you are looking for

R

Rabbit vol.8-8, *see also* Mammal
Racoon vol.8-9, *see also* Mammal
Radio vol.2-45; vol.8-10, *see also* Communication, Television
Railway vol.8-11, *see also* Train, Transport
Rain *see* Water cycle, Weather
Rainbow vol.8-12, *see also* Colour, Light
Rainforest vol.3-43; vol.4-21, 36; vol.5-15; vol.6-15; vol.7-5, 6, 7, 25; vol.8-13, 38, *see also* Forest, Plant

vol. 8–10 means look on page 10 of volume 8

see also references tell you about other entries related to this one

see references tell you where to look to find information

Remember: the volume number is followed by a hyphen, and then by the page number.

The Subject Index

The main subject headings are in Dewey Decimal order, like books in libraries.

WORLD RELIGIONS

Buddhism
Cathedral
Christianity
Hinduism
Islam
Judaism
Sikhism

TRANSPORT

Aeroplane
Balloon
Barge
Bicycle
Bus
Canoe
Car
Helicopter
Hovercraft
Motorcycle
Railway
Ship
Submarine
Train
Truck
Waterway

PLANTS

Cactus
Endangered
    species
Fern
Flower
Forest
Fungus
Leaf
Life cycle
Moss
Photosynthesis
Root
Seed
Stem
Tree
Wood

DINOSAURS

Brachiosaur
Pterosaur
Stegosaur
Triceratops
Tyrannosaur

ANIMALS

Amphibians

Frog
Toad

Birds

Chicken
Crane
Duck
Eagle
Emu
Flamingo
Goose
Gull
Hawk
Hummingbird
Kiwi
Migration
Ostrich
Owl
Parrot
Penguin
Pigeon
Seabird
Swan
Vulture
Woodpecker

Crustaceans

Crab
Woodlouse

Fish

Eel
Migration
Ray
Sea horse
Shark
Tropical fish

Insects

Ant
Bee
Beetle
Butterfly
Caterpillar
Cockroach
Dragonfly
Earwig
Firefly
Flea
Fly
Grasshopper
Ladybird
Lice
Mosquito
Moth
Praying mantis
Termite
Wasp

Mammals

Aardvark
Anteater
Antelope
Ape
Badger
Bat
Bear
Beaver
Bison
Buffalo
Camel
Cat
Cattle
Cheetah
Coyote
Deer
Dog
Dolphin
Elephant
Fox
Giraffe
Goat
Hare
Hedgehog
Hippopotamus
Horse
Jaguar
Kangaroo
Koala
Leopard
Lion
Marsupial
Monkey
Moose
Mouse
Opossum
Otter
Panda
Pig
Platypus
Porcupine
Rabbit
Racoon
Rat
Rhinoceros
Sea lion
Seal
Sheep
Skunk
Squirrel
Tiger
Whale
Wolf
Wolverine
Zebra

Molluscs

Octopus
Slug
Snail
Squid

Reptiles

Alligator
Crocodile
Lizard
Snake
Tortoise
Turtle

Nocturnal animals

Aardvark
Badger
Bat
Cat
Centipede
Cockroach
Coyote
Earwig
Firefly
Fox
Frog
Hare
Hedgehog
Hippopotamus
Kiwi
Koala
Moth
Opossum
Owl
Racoon
Slug
Toad

SCIENCE AND TECHNOLOGY

Air
Bacteria
Bar code
Blood
Calendar
Camera
Colour
Comet
Communication
Computer
Day and Night
Drug
Ear
Egg
Electricity
Energy
Engine
Eye
Food chain
Fuel
Heart
Heat
Hibernation

SCIENCE AND TECHNOLOGY

continued ...

Human body
Internet
Laser
Life cycle
Light
Lung
Machines, simple
Magnet
Matter
Measurement
Metal
Metamorphosis
Meteor
Moon
Numbers
Nutrition
Oxygen
Planet
Plastic
Pollution
Radio
Rainbow
Robot
Skeleton
Smell
Solar system
Sound
Space
    exploration
Spacecraft
Star
Sun
Taste
Telephone
Television
Time
Tooth
Touch
Virus

THE ARTS

Art

Architecture
Painting
Sculpture

Literature

Alphabet
Fable
Fairy tale
Hieroglyphics
Legend
Myth
Poetry
Story

Music

Classical music
Folk music
Jazz
Musical
    instrument
Orchestra
Percussion
    instruments
Pop music
Stringed
    instruments
Wind
    instruments

Performing arts

Ballet
Dance
Drama
Opera
Puppetry
Theatre

GEOGRAPHY

Aborigines
Africa
Antarctica
Arctic
Asia
Australasia
Aztecs
Bay
Climate
Coast
Continent
Coral
Crop
Delta
Desert
Earth
Earthquake
Europe
Farming
Flood
Home
Hurricane
Incas
Island
Lake
Lightning
Map
Maya
Mining
Mountain
Native
    Americans
North America
Ocean
Peninsula
Port
Rainforest
River
Rocks
Season
Soil
South America
Tornado
Tundra
Valley
Volcano
Water
Water cycle
Weather

COUNTRIES

Africa

Algeria
Botswana
Chad
Democratic
    Republic
    of Congo
Egypt
Ethiopia
Ghana
Kenya
Libya
Madagascar
Morocco
Nigeria
Rwanda
Somalia
South Africa
Sudan
Tunisia
Uganda
Zambia
Zimbabwe

Asia

Afghanistan
Bangladesh
Cambodia
China
India
Indonesia
Iran
Iraq
Israel
Japan
Jordan
Kuwait
Lebanon
Malaysia
Nepal
North Korea
Pakistan
Philippines
Saudi Arabia
Singapore
South Korea
Sri Lanka
Syria
Taiwan
Thailand
Turkey
Vietnam

Australasia

Australia
New Zealand
Papua New
    Guinea

Europe

Albania
Austria
Belgium
Bosnia-
    Hercegovina
Bulgaria
Croatia
Czech Republic
Denmark
England
Finland
France
Germany
Greece
Hungary
Iceland
Ireland
Italy
Luxembourg
Netherlands
Northern
    Ireland
Norway
Poland
Portugal
Romania
Russia

Scotland
Slovakia
Slovenia
Spain
Sweden
Switzerland
Turkey
Ukraine
United
    Kingdom
Wales
Yugoslavia

North America

Bahamas
Barbados
Belize
Canada
Costa Rica
Cuba
Dominican
    Republic
El Salvador
Guatemala
Haiti
Honduras
Jamaica
Mexico
Nicaragua
Panama
Puerto Rico
United States of
    America

COUNTRIES
continued ...

South America

Argentina
Bolivia
Brazil
Chile
Colombia
Ecuador
Peru
Trinidad and Tobago
Venezuela

HISTORY

Bronze Age
Castle
Cathedral
China, Ancient
Egypt, Ancient
Greece, Ancient
Hieroglyphics
Industrial revolution
Iron Age
Knight
Middle Ages
Olympic Games
Pyramid
Rome, Ancient
Stone Age
Vikings
World War I
World War II

The alphabetic index

Remember: the volume number is followed by a hyphen, and then by the page number

Bedouin vol.5-33
Bee vol.1-43, *see also* Insect, Wasp
Beetle vol.1-44; vol.5-17, *see also* Insect, Ladybird
Belgium vol.1-45, *see also* Europe
Belize vol.1-46, *see also* Maya, North America
Bell, Alexander Graham vol.2-45, vol.9-38
Bible vol.2-18, 37
Bicycle vol.1-47, *see also* Motorcycle, Transport
Bidpai vol.4-5
Bird vol.1-48; vol.3-36; vol, 6-6, 29, *see also* Animal, Seabird
Bird of prey vol.3-29; vol.4-40
Bison vol.2-4; vol.6-46, *see also* Buffalo, Mammal
Black Sea vol.2-14; vol.10-17
Blood vol.2-5; vol.4-41, *see also* Heart, Human body
Blood donor vol.2-5
Blue whale vol.6-18
Bohemia *see* Czech Republic
Bolivia vol.2-6, *see also* South America
Bombay vol.5-14
Bone vol.3-30; vol.8-45; vol.10-23
Borneo vol.6-17
Bosnia-Hercegovina vol.2-7, *see also* Europe, Yugoslavia
Botswana vol.2-8, *see also* Africa
Brachiosaur vol.2-9; vol.3-21, *see also* Dinosaur, Fossil
Braille vol.10-4
Bratislava vol.8-47
Brazil vol.2-10, *see also* Rainforest, South America
Breathing vol.5-8; vol.6-12
Bronze vol.2-11; vol.6-24
Bronze Age vol.2-11, *see also* Iron Age, Stone Age
Buddhism vol.2-12; vol.5-14; vol.9-41, *see also* India
Buffalo vol.2-13; vol.9-41, *see also* Bison, Mammal
Bulgaria vol.2-14, *see also* Europe
Bus vol.2-15, *see also* Transport
Butterfly vol.2-16; vol.6-25, *see also* Caterpillar, Metamorphosis

C

Cactus vol.2-17; vol.3-20, *see also* Desert, Plant
Calcutta vol.5-14
Calendar vol.2-18, *see also* Season, Time
Calorie vol.7-12
Cambodia vol.2-19, *see also* Asia
Camel vol.2-20, *see also* Desert, Mammal
Camera vol.2-21, *see also* Light, Television
Canada vol.2-22, *see also* Native Americans, North America
Canal vol.1-38; vol.10-33
Canoe vol.2-23, *see also* Native Americans, Transport
Canyon vol.10-21
Car vol.2-24, 46; vol.3-45; vol.9-11, *see also* Engine, Transport
Caracas vol.10-22
Carbon dioxide vol.1-9; vol.6-12; vol.7-34
Cargo ship vol.7-46; vol.8-42
Caribbean Sea vol.7-7
Caribou vol.1-22; vol.3-16
Carnivore vol.1-15; vol.4-20; vol.9-46
Carthage vol.10-12
Cartilage vol.10-23
Castle vol.2-25, *see also* Knight, Middle Ages
Cat vol.2-26, *see also* Leopard, Lion, Tiger
Caterpillar vol.2-16, 27; vol.6-39, *see also* Butterfly, Metamorphosis, Moth
Catfish vol.10-4
Cathedral vol.1-21; vol.2-28, *see also* Christianity, Middle Ages
Cattle vol.2-29, *see also* Farming, Mammal
CD player vol.5-44
CD-ROM vol.2-46
Cello vol.9-28
Centipede vol.2-30, *see also* Invertebrate
Ceylon *see* Sri Lanka

Chad vol.2-31, *see also* Africa
Chalk vol.4-22; vol.8-21
Chameleon vol.6-11
Chart vol.6-19
Cheetah vol.2-32, *see also* Cat, Mammal
Cheque vol.6-32
Chewing gum vol.4-36
Chicken vol.2-23, *see also* Bird
Chile vol.2-34; vol.5-13, *see also* South America
Chimpanzee vol.1-20
China vol.1-47; vol.2-35, *see also* Asia, China (Ancient)
China, Ancient vol.2-36, *see also* China
Chinese opera vol.7-16
Chlorophyll vol.5-45; vol.7-34
Choreographer vol.1-33
Christianity vol.2-37; vol.6-28, *see also* Cathedral
Chrysalis vol.6-39
Clam vol.6-31
Clarinet vol.10-36
Classical music vol.2-38, *see also* Music, Musical instrument
Clay vol.9-8
Climate vol.2-39, *see also* Season, Weather
Coal vol.3-40, 44; vol.4-22, 26; vol.5-16; vol.6-30
Coast vol.2-40, *see also* Bay, Delta, Ocean, Peninsula
Cockroach vol.2-41, *see also* Insect
Cocoa vol.4-29
Cod vol.3-36
Coffee vol.2-42; vol.3-4, 47
Colombia vol.2-42, *see also* South America
Colour vol.2-43; vol.8-12, *see also* Light, Television
Columbus, Christopher vol.3-12, 24; vol.10-22
Comedy vol.3-26
Comet vol.2-44; vol.6-26; vol. 9-9, *see also* Meteor, Planet, Solar system, Sun
Commonwealth vol.10-18

Remember: the volume number is followed by a hyphen, and then by the page number.

Communication vol.2-45, *see also* Computer, Internet, Radio, Telephone, Television

Commuter vol.10-6

Computer vol.1-37; vol.2-46; vol.5-18; vol.6-36; vol.8-20, *see also* Bar code, Laser

Condor vol.9-13

Conductor (orchestra) vol.7-18

Confucius vol.7-8

Consonant vol.1-13

Constellation vol.9-22

Continent vol.2-47, *see also* Earth, Ocean

Copernicus vol.9-9

Copper vol.2-11; vol.6-24; vol.10-46

Coral vol.2-48; vol.6-15; vol.8-33

Cormorant vol.8-36

Costa Rica vol.3-4, *see also* North America

Costume, traditional *see* entries for individual countries

Cotton vol.3-10; vol.5-16

Coyote vol.3-5, 22, *see also* Dog, Mammal, Wolf

Crab vol.3-6, 11; vol.5-19; vol.8-33, *see also* Crustacean, Sea life

Crafts *see* entries for individual countries

Crane vol.3-7, *see also* Bird

Crater vol.6-26, 34

Credit card vol.6-32

Creole vol.1-46; vol.4-38

Croatia vol.3-8, *see also* Yugoslavia

Crocodile vol.1-26; vol.3-9, 36; vol.8-16, *see also* Alligator, Reptile

Crop vol.3-10; vol.4-7; vol.8-38; vol.10-21, *see also* Farming, and entries for individual countries and crops

Crustacean vol.3-11; vol.8-33, *see also* Animal, Sea life

Cuba vol.3-12, *see also* Island, North America

Cuneiform writing vol.6-10

Cyrillic alphabet vol.2-7

Czech Republic vol.3-13, *see also* Europe, Slovakia

Czechoslovakia *see* Slovakia, Czech Republic

D

Dam vol.3-40; vol.4-16; vol.10-31

Dance vol.3-14, *see also* Ballet, Music

Day and night vol.3-15, *see also* Earth, Season

Deer vol.3-16, *see also* Mammal, Antelope

Delta vol.3-17, *see also* Coast, River

Democratic Republic of Congo (DRC) vol.3-18, *see also* Africa

Denmark vol.3-19, *see also* Europe

Desert vol.3-20; vol.8-38, *see also* Cactus, Camel, Climate

Diamond vol.6-23, 30

Didgeridoo vol.10-36

Diesel engine vol.10-10

Digestive system vol.5-8

Dingo vol.1-26; vol.3-22

Dinosaur vol.3-21; vol.4-22, *see also* Fossil, Reptile

Disease vol.4-18; vol.8-14; vol.10-26

Dog vol.3-22; vol.9-5; vol.10-23, *see also* Coyote, Mammal, Wolf

Dolphin vol.3-23, *see also* Mammal

Dominican Republic vol.3-24, *see also* Island, North America

Dove vol.7-36

Dracula vol.8-22

Dragonfly vol.3-25, *see also* Insect

Drama vol.3-26, *see also* Literature

Dreamtime vol.1-5

Drought vol.3-47

Drug vol.3-27, *see also* Human body

Drum vol.7-31

Duck vol.3-28; vol.8-36, *see also* Bird

Dung beetle vol.1-44

E

E-mail (electronic mail) vol.2-45; vol.5-18; vol.9-38

Eagle vol.3-29, *see also* Bird, Hawk

Ear vol.3-30, *see also* Human body, Sound

Earth vol.3-15, 31; vol.6-7, 16; vol.7-37; vol.9-9, *see also* Planet, Solar system, Weather

Earthquake vol.3-32; vol.5-30; vol.7-5, 32, *see also* Earth, Volcano

Earwig vol.3-33, *see also* Insect

Echo vol.9-11

Echo location vol.3-23

Ecuador vol.3-34; vol.5-13, *see also* Incas, South America

Eel vol.3-35, *see also* Fish

Egg vol.3-36; vol.6-6 *see also* Bird, and entries for individual animals

Egypt vol.3-37, *see also* Africa, Egypt (Ancient), Pyramid

Egypt, Ancient vol.3-38; vol.4-46; vol.6-23; vol.8-7, 42, *see also* Egypt, Hieroglyphics, Pyramid

Eiffel Tower vol.4-24

Eire *see* Ireland

El Salvador vol.3-39, *see also* North America

Electricity vol.3-40, 44, 45; vol.4-26; vol.6-7, 41; vol.8-18; vol.10-31, 32, 34, *see also* Energy, Heat, Light

Electronic keyboard vol.7-18

Elephant vol.3-30, 41, *see also* Mammal

Elk vol.6-35

Emu vol.3-42, *see also* Australia, Bird

Endangered species vol.3-43, *see also* Animal, Plant

Energy vol.3-44; vol.6-7, 8; vol.7-12; vol.10-32, *see also* Electricity, Heat, Light

Engine vol.3-45; 10-5, 10, *see also* Car, Electricity, Transport

England vol.3-46, *see also* Northern Ireland, Scotland, United Kingdom, Wales

English language vol.5-43
Erosion vol.2-40; vol.9-8
Ethiopia vol.3-47; vol.5-4,
   see also Africa
Eucalyptus vol.4-21; vol.5-39
Europe vol.2-47; vol.3-48, *see
   also* Continent
European Union (EU) vol.1-45;
   vol.3-48
Exoskeleton vol.8-45
Eye vol.4-4, *see also* Animal,
   Human body

F

Fable vol.4-5, *see also* Literature,
   Story
Fairy tale vol.4-6, *see also*
   Literature, Story
Farming vol.4-7; vol.8-38;
   vol.9-8; vol.10-21, *see also*
   Crop, Soil, Weather, and entries
   for individual countries
Fax vol.2-45; vol.9-38
Feather vol.1-48
Fern vol.4-8, 21, *see also* Plant
Fertilizer vol.3-10; vol.4-7;
   vol.9-8
Festivals *see* Calendar, and entries
   for individual countries and
   religions
Finland vol.4-9, *see also* Arctic,
   Europe
Firefly vol.4-10, *see also* Beetle,
   Insect
Fish vol.4-11, *see also* Fish
   (tropical), Sea life
Fish (tropical) vol.4-12, *see also*
   Coral, Fish, Sea life
Fishing vol.2-40; vol.5-12
Flag vol.4-13, *see also*
   Communication
Flamingo vol.4-14, *see also* Bird
Flax vol.1-45; vol.7-9
Flea vol.4-15, *see also* Insect
Flood vol.3-17; vol.4-16, *see also*
   Coast, River, Weather
Flower vol.4-17, *see also* Plant,
   Seed
Fly vol.4-18, *see also* Insect,
   Mosquito

Folk music vol.4-19, *see also*
   Dance, Music, Musical
   instrument
Food *see* entries for individual
   countries
Food chain vol.4-20, *see also*
   Animal, Energy, Plant
Food-poisoning vol.4-18
Football vol.3-48
Forest vol.4-21; vol.10-7, *see also*
   Rainforest, Tree, Wood
Formosa *see* Taiwan
Fossil vol.4-22, *see also* Dinosaur,
   Fuel
Fossil fuel vol.4-22, 26
Fox vol.4-23, *see also* Dog,
   Mammal
France vol.4-24, *see also* Europe
Franklin, Benjamin vol.6-8
French horn vol.10-36
French Revolution vol.4-24
Frequency vol.8-10
Frog vol.1-14; vol.4-25, 45,
   see also Amphibian,
   Metamorphosis
Fuel vol.4-26, 42, *see also*
   Electricity, Energy
Fungus vol.4-27, *see also* Plant

G

Galaxy vol.9-22
Gas vol.6-21
Gas, natural vol.3-40; vol.4-26;
   vol.5-40; vol.6-4, 7, 30;
   vol.7-10
Gecko vol.8-16
German Democratic Republic
   see Germany
German Federal Republic
   see Germany
Germany vol.4-28; vol.10-42, 43,
   see also Europe
Ghana vol.4-29, *see also* Africa
Gibbon vol.1-20
Gilbert and Sullivan vol.7-16
Gillespie, Dizzy vol.6-43
Giraffe vol.4-30, *see also*
   Mammal
Glacier vol.5-12
Glass vol.3-13
Globe vol.6-19

Globe Theatre vol.9-42
Glow-worm vol.4-10
Goat vol.4-31, *see also* Mammal
Gods and goddesses vol.1-29;
   vol.3-38; vol.4-35, 47; vol.5-13;
   vol.6-22, 45
Gold vol.6-24, 30
Gold Coast vol.4-29
Goose vol.4-32; vol.8-36, *see also*
   Bird
Gorge vol.10-21
Gorilla vol.1-20; vol.8-26
Graphite vol.1-28
Grasshopper vol.3-30; vol.4-33;
   vol.6-6, 25, *see also* Insect
Gravity vol.9-9, 31
Great Britain vol.10-18
Great Wall of China vol.2-35, 36
Greece vol.4-34, *see also* Europe,
   Greece (Ancient)
Greece (Ancient) vol.4-35;
   vol.6-45; vol.7-15; vol.8-30;
   vol.9-42, *see also* Greece,
   Olympic Games
Greek alphabet vol.3-17
Greenland vol.1-22; vol.5-25
Grimm brothers vol.4-6
Guatemala vol.4-36, *see also*
   Maya, North America
Guinea pig vol.3-34
Guitar vol.6-44; vol.9-28
Gulf States vol.5-40
Gulf stream vol.5-12; vol.7-13
Gulf War vol.5-21
Gull vol.4-37; vol.8-36; vol.10-23,
   see also Bird, Seabird
Guru Granth Sahib vol. 8-43
Guru Nanak vol.8-43

H

Hailstone vol.10-34
Haiti vol.4-38, *see also* Island,
   North America
Hale/Bopp comet vol.2-44
Haley, Bill vol.7-44
Halley's Comet vol.2-44
Hare vol.3-30; vol.4-39, *see also*
   Mammal, Rabbit
Hawaiian islands vol.5-25
Hawk vol.4-40, *see also* Bird
Healthy Eating Pyramid vol.7-12

Heart vol.2-5; vol.4-41; vol.5-8, *see also* Blood, Human body, Lung

Heat vol.3-44; vol.4-42, *see also* Energy, Fuel

Hedgehog vol.4-43, 45, *see also* Mammal

Helicopter vol.4-44, *see also* Aeroplane, Transport

Hendrix, Jimi vol.6-44

Herbivore vol.1-15; vol.4-20; vol.9-46

Hercegovina *see* Bosnia-Hercegovina

Hibernation vol.1-39, 41; vol.4-45; vol.8-38, *see also* Animal, Season

Hieroglyphics vol.1-29; vol.3-38; vol.4-46; vol.6-22, *see also* Alphabet, Aztecs, Egypt (Ancient), Maya

Himalaya Mountains vol.1-25; vol.2-35; vol.5-14; vol.6-41, 47

Hinduism vol.4-47; vol.5-14; vol.6-47, *see also* India

Hippopotamus vol.4-48, *see also* Mammal

Hispaniola vol.3-24; vol.4-38

Holland *see* Netherlands

Holocaust vol.5-34

Hologram vol.5-44

Home vol.5-4, *see also* Architecture

Honduras vol.3-39; vol.5-5, *see also* North America

Honey vol.1-43

Hong Kong vol.1-25

Hornet vol.10-30

Horse vol.5-6, *see also* Mammal, Transport

Hovercraft vol.5-7, *see also* Transport

Human body vol.5-8; vol.10-31, *see also* Ear, Eye, Heart

Hummingbird vol.3-36; vol.5-9, *see also* Bird, Migration

Hungary vol.5-10, *see also* Europe

Hurricane vol.1-36; vol.5-11; vol.10-34, *see also* Climate, Tornado, Weather

Hutu vol.8-26

Hydro-electric power vol.10-32

I

Ice vol.6-21

Iceland vol.5-12, *see also* Arctic, Europe

Iguana vol.6-11

Immunization vol.10-26

Incas vol.5-13, *see also* Aztecs, Maya, South America

India vol.5-14; vol.6-43, *see also* Asia

Indian Ocean vol.1-8; vol.7-13

Indonesia vol.1-25; vol.5-15; vol.7-18, *see also* Asia

Industrial revolution vol.5-16, *see also* United Kingdom

Industry *see* entries for individual countries

Insect vol.4-45; vol.5-17, 19; vol.6-6, 25, *see also* Animal, Invertebrate, Metamorphosis

Insectivore vol.1-15

Insulation vol.3-44; vol.4-42

Internal combustion engine vol.3-45

Internet vol.5-18; vol.6-10; vol.9-38, *see also* Communication, Computer, Telephone

Inuit vol.2-22, 23; vol.10-11

Invertebrate vol.5-19, *see also* Crustacean, Insect, Mollusc, Vertebrate

Iran vol.5-20, 21, *see also* Asia, Islam

Iraq vol.5-21, *see also* Asia

Ireland vol.5-22, *see also* Europe, Northern Ireland

Iron Age vol.5-23, *see also* Bronze Age, Stone Age

Islam vol.5-20, 24; vol.7-24; vol.8-27; vol.9-35

Island vol.5-25, *see also* Coast, Coral, Ocean

Israel vol.5-26, *see also* Asia

Italy vol.5-27; vol.7-30, *see also* Europe, Rome (Ancient)

J

Jackal vol.3-22

Jackrabbit *see* Hare

Jaguar vol.5-28, *see also* Cat, Leopard

Jamaica vol.5-29, *see also* North America

Japan vol.1-25; vol.5-30; vol.8-6; vol.10-43, *see also* Asia, Earthquake

Java vol.8-6

Jazz vol.5-31, *see also* Music, Musical instrument

Jellyfish vol.5-19, 32, *see also* Invertebrate, Sea Life

Jerusalem vol.5-26, 34

Jesus Christ vol.2-37

Jews *see* Judaism

Jordan vol.5-33, *see also* Asia

Judaism vol.5-34, *see also* Israel, World War II

Jupiter vol.7-37; vol.9-9

K

Kalahari Desert vol.1-8; vol.2-8

Kangaroo vol.1-26; vol.5-35; vol.6-20, *see also* Australia, Mammal, Marsupial

Karakoram Mountains vol.6-41

Kenya vol.5-36, *see also* Africa

Khrishna vol.4-47

King Arthur vol.5-47

Kiwi vol.1-26; vol.5-37; vol.7-4, *see also* Bird, New Zealand

Knight vol.5-38, *see also* Castle, Middle Ages

Koala vol.1-26; vol.5-39, *see also* Australia, Mammal, Marsupial

Komodo dragon vol.5-15; vol.6-11

Krill vol.1-17; vol.8-40

Kuwait vol.5-21, 40, *see also* Asia, Desert, Fuel

Remember: the volume number is followed by a hyphen, and then by the page number.

L

La Fontaine, Jean vol.4–5

Ladybird vol.5–41, *see also* Beetle, Insect

Lake vol.5–42, *see also* River, Valley

Language vol.5–43, *see also* Alphabet, Communication, and entries for individual countries

Lapland vol.4–9

Lapps vol.10–11

Laser vol.1–37; vol.5–44, *see also* Bar code, Computer, Light

Lava vol.10–27

Leaf vol.5–45; vol.7–34, *see also* Photosynthesis, Plant

Lebanon vol.5–46, *see also* Asia

Leech vol.10–44

Legend vol.5–47, *see also* Literature, Myth, Story

Lemur vol.6–15

Leonardo da Vinci vol.7–23

Leopard vol.5–48, *see also* Cat, Mammal

Lessing, Gotthold Ephraim vol.4–5

Lever vol.6–14

Libya vol.6–4, *see also* Africa, Desert

Lice vol.6–5, *see also* Insect

Life cycle vol.6–6, *see also* Flower, Metamorphosis

Light pollution vol.7–43

Light vol.3–44; vol.6–7, 34; vol.9–22, *see also* Climate, Energy, Heat, Sun

Lightning vol.6–8; vol.10–34, *see also* Electricity, Weather

Lion vol.4–20; vol.6–9, *see also* Africa, Cat, Mammal

Liquid vol.6–21

Literature vol.6–10, *see also* Alphabet, Drama, Poem, Story

Livingstone, David vol.10–46

Lizard vol.1–15; vol.6–11; vol.8–16, *see also* Reptile

Llama vol.3–34

Lobster vol.3–11; vol.5–19

Loch Ness vol.5–42; vol.8–29

Locust vol.5–17

London vol.3–46; vol.10–6, 18, 43

Longfellow, Henry Wadsworth vol.7–41

Longhouse vol.6–46; vol.7–33

Longship vol.10–25

Lorry *see* Truck

Lung vol.5–8; vol.6–12, *see also* Air, Human body, Oxygen

Luxembourg vol.6–13, *see also* Europe

M

Machines, simple vol.6–14, *see also* Energy

Machu Picchu vol.5–13

Madagascar vol.6–15, *see also* Africa, Island

Maggot vol.4–18

Magma vol.8–21; vol.10–27

Magnet vol.6–16

Maize vol.2–42; vol.3–10, 39; vol.5–5

Makkah vol.5–24; vol.8–27

Malaria vol.4–18

Malaysia vol.6–17, *see also* Asia, Rainforest

Malnutrition vol.7–12

Mammal vol.3–36; vol.6–18, *see also* Animal, Vertebrate

Mandela, Nelson vol.9–12

Manta ray vol.8–15

Maori vol.6–45; vol.7–4

Map vol.6–19

Marconi, Guglielmo vol.8–10

Marianas Trench vol.7–13

Marionette vol.8–6

Mars vol.7–37; vol.9–9, 15; vol.10–27

Marsh Arabs vol.5–21

Marsupial vol.6–20, *see also* Australia, Kangaroo, Koala, Opossum

Matter vol.6–21, *see also* Temperature

Maya vol.1–46; vol.4–36, 46; vol.6–22; vol.8–7, *see also* Aztecs, Hieroglyphics, Incas

Measurement vol.6–23, *see also* Calendar, Numbers, Time

Medicine vol.3–27; vol.5–45

Mediterranean Sea vol.3–48; vol.4–34

Mercury vol.7–37; vol.9–9

Metal vol.6–24, *see also* Rock

Metamorphosis vol.6–25, *see also* Amphibian, Insect, Life cycle

Meteor vol.6–26, *see also* Earth, Planet, Solar system

Meteorite vol.6–26

Metric system vol.6–23

Mexico vol.6–27; vol.7–7, *see also* Aztecs, Maya, North America

Microchip vol.2–46

Middle Ages vol.2–25, 28; vol.5–38; vol.6–28, *see also* Castle, Cathedral, Knight

Middle East vol.5–33; vol.5–46

Migration vol.6–29; vol.8–38, *see also* Animal

Milne, A.A. vol.7–41

Mineral vol.8–21

Mining vol.1–8; vol.6–30; vol.9–12; vol.10–16, *see also* Metal, Rock

Mississippi delta vol.3–17

Mollusc vol.6–31, *see also* Animal, Invertebrate

Money vol.6–32, *see also* Metal, and entries for individual countries

Mongols vol.2–36

Monkey vol.1–15, 20, 25; vol.6–33, *see also* Ape, Mammal

Monsoon vol.1–35; vol.7–33

Montenegro vol.10–45

Monteverdi, Claudio vol.7–18

Moon vol.6–34; vol.9–9, 16, *see also* Earth, Solar system, Space exploration, Sun

Moose vol.6–35, *see also* Arctic, Deer, Tundra

Morocco vol.6–36, *see also* Africa, Desert

Moscow vol.8–25

Mosquito vol.4–18; vol.6–37, *see also* Fly, Insect

Moss vol.6–38, *see also* Plant

Moth vol.6–39, *see also* Butterfly, Caterpillar, Insect, Metamorphosis

Mother Teresa vol.1–10

Motor racing vol.4–13

Plastics vol.7-39, *see also* Heat, Mining

Platypus vol.6-18; vol.7-40, *see also* Australia, Mammal

Pluto vol.7-37; vol.9-9

Poetry vol.7-41, *see also* Literature

Poland vol.7-42, *see also* Europe

Polar bear vol.1-22, 45; vol.6-18

Police vol.3-46

Pollen vol.1-43; vol.4-17; vol.6-6

Pollution vol.1-9; vol.3-45; vol.6-12; vol.7-13, 43; vol.8-22, *see also* Water cycle

Polyp vol.2-48; vol.5-32

Pop music vol.3-14; vol.7-44, *see also* Music, Musical instrument

Population *see* entries for individual continents and countries

Porcupine vol.7-45, *see also* Mammal

Port vol.7-46, *see also* Bay, Coast, Ship

Portugal vol.7-47, *see also* Europe

Power station vol.3-40, 44; vol.6-41

Praying mantis vol.7-48, *see also* Insect, Invertebrate

Pteranodon vol.8-4

Pterodactyl vol.8-4

Pterosaur vol.8-4, *see also* Dinosaur, Fossil

Puerto Rico vol.8-5, *see also* North America, United States of America

Puffin vol.8-36

Pulley vol.6-14

Punch and Judy vol.8-6

Puppetry vol.8-6, *see also* Drama, Theatre

Pygmy vol.3-18; vol.8-26

Pyramid vol.3-37, 38; vol.6-22; vol.8-7, *see also* Egypt, Egypt (Ancient), Maya

Pythagoras vol.6-43

Remember: the volume number is followed by a hyphen, and then by the page number.

Q

Qur'an vol.5-24

R

Rabbit vol.8-8, *see also* Mammal

Racoon vol.8-9, *see also* Mammal

Radio vol.2-45; vol.8-10, *see also* Communication, Television

Railway vol.8-11, *see also* Train, Transport

Rain *see* Water cycle, Weather

Rainbow vol.8-12, *see also* Colour, Light

Rainforest vol.3-43; vol.4-21, 36; vol.5-15; vol.6-15; vol.7-5, 6, 7, 25; vol.8-13, 38, *see also* Forest, Plant

Ramp vol.6-14

Rat vol.8-14, *see also* Mammal

Ray vol.8-15, *see also* Fish, Sea life

Recycling vol.7-39

Refraction vol.6-7

Reggae music vol.5-29

Reindeer vol.1-22; vol.4-9

Rembrandt vol.6-48

Renaissance vol.6-28

Reptile vol.3-36; vol.4-45; vol.6-6; vol.8-16, *see also* Animal

Reservoir vol.5-42; vol.6-41; vol.10-31

Respiratory system vol.5-8; vol.6-12

Rhinoceros vol.3-43; vol.8-17, *see also* Mammal

Rhythm vol.3-14; vol.7-41, 44

Rice vol.2-35; vol.3-10, 18, 39; vol.4-7

River vol.8-18, *see also* Delta, Flood, Valley, and entries for individual countries

Road vol.8-19, *see also* Transport

Robot vol.8-20; vol.9-15, *see also* Computer, Laser

Rock and roll vol.7-44

Rocks vol.8-21, *see also* Mining

Rocky Mountains vol.7-7; vol.10-20

Roman alphabet vol.2-7

Roman Catholicism vol.7-32; vol.8-5

Roman Empire vol.3-38; vol.4-35; vol.8-23

Romania vol.8-22, *see also* Europe

Rome, Ancient vol.6-45; vol.8-19, 23, 30, *see also* Italy, Road

Root vol.8-24, 39, *see also* Plant

Rubber vol.2-10; vol.6-17; vol.7-46

Russia vol.7-18; vol.8-15, *see also* Asia, Europe

Rwanada vol.8-26, *see also* Africa

S

Sahara Desert vol.1-8, 11; vol.3-20

St Patrick vol.5-22

Salmon vol.6-29

Salt vol.6-30

San Francisco vol.1-40; vol.2-24; vol.3-32

Satellite vol.2-45; vol.8-10; vol.9-15, 16, 38, 39

Saturn vol.6-34; vol.7-37; vol.9-9

Saudi Arabai vol.8-27, *see also* Asia

Savanna vol.1-8

School of the Air vol.1-27

Scorpion vol.8-28, *see also* Invertebrate

Scotland vol.8-29, *see also* Europe, United Kingdom

Screw vol.6-14

Sculpture vol.1-24; vol.8-30, *see also* Art

Sea anemone vol.8-31, *see also* Sea life

Sea horse vol.8-32, *see also* Fish

Sea life vol.8-33, *see also* Coast, Coral, Fish

Sea lion vol.8-34, *see also* Mammal, Sea life

Sea pollution vol.7-13, 43

Sea urchin vol.8-35, *see also* Sea life

Seabird vol.8-36, *see also* Bird, Gull

Remember: the volume number is followed by a hyphen, and then by the page number.